# WITH CHERRIES ON TOP

Poetry by

AVA ROULIER

Taylor and Seale Publishing, LLC
Daytona Beach Shores,
Florida

Contact: Mary Custureri, Ed.D., President

**Taylor and Seale Publishing, LLC.**

*2 Oceans West Boulevard, Unit 406*
*Daytona Beach Shores, Florida 32118*

*Phone: 888-866-8248*

*Email: Customersupport@TaylorandSeale.com*

ISBN: 978-1-940224-72-5

Cover layout by WhiteRabbitGraphix.com

Photography by fulcosfotos@cl.rr.com

# Dedication

This book is dedicated to my beloved grandfather
and  fellow poet, Daniel Pels, whom I
affectionately call Papa.

## ABOUT AVA

Ava Roulier, who is now nine years old, started writing poetry with her grandfather, Dan Pels when she was five years old.

Several poems in this book were written on her own when she was seven.

Ava is immersed in many forms of art: painting, poetry, piano and gymnastics, excelling in all four. Her parents, Ken and Laurie, are very proud of her.

Ava had her first public and very successful poetry recital at the HUB in New Smyrna Beach, Florida on April 16, 2014.

Ava's grandfather, Dan Pels, is a published poet in his own right. He also sponsors poetry presentations in his popular poetry nights throughout Daytona. Ava's grandmother is an accomplished musician and teaches piano. Even her younger brother has begun to compete with Ava in painting and poetry.

Ava Roulier

# Where My Ideas Come From
## Ava Roulier

I get ideas for my poems in many ways. One of my major inspirations is nature and watching the world around me. Often, I like to sit in my back yard where it's peaceful and watch the trees. One of my poems is Peppermint Tree. I got that idea from doing what I just told you: going out in nature and coming up with ideas. I was looking at the trees and watching how they dance around in the breeze. Once I get a thought stuck in my head, I get my pen or pencil and write, write, write!!

I like to read and I get ideas from reading. One of my favorite authors is Roald Dahl.
I love the characters in his books because they all have different or funny traits about them that make me think about different ideas. I particularly liked Farmer Boggis, who eats everything and Farmer Beans, who only drinks apple cider in the *Fantastic Mr. Fox.*

I like to write with my grandpa because he's a really good poet and he would sometimes say a word or a sentence that would make me think maybe I could write a poem about that.   My brother, Logan, writes poems too. His poems are so silly that my grandpa can't stop laughing. One time he was laughing so hard with a knife in his hands that I got worried and asked him to give me the knife.  That line, "give me the knife", became the end of Logan's poem. That encouraged me to write about the same subject in way different words.   You just never know what will give you an idea for a poem!

I also like to play with words. Once I start thinking and rhyming, I can probably come up with a cool poem. You can too! Just give it a try!

# CONTENTS

## Thoughts

## Observations

# Fun and Laughter

THOUGHTS

# HAPPY WORLD

When the birds
are in flight
the sky is blue.
The sun
is shining bright.

When you see
the sky as bright
as flowers,
you will happily see
the world
all around you.

# FLOWER CAMP

fancy petals
flower power
full of scent
and pollen
carrying
more flowers


# IF I CAN'T

I want to go to school so bad
If I can't, I'll feel so sad.
I'll sleep in a pile of rocks
without my socks
and my head in a bag.

# A HAPPY PLACE

The place of nowhere
The place of nowhere
is the place
I know.

The place of nowhere,
The place of nowhere
has ice cream cake
and snow.

# OH TO BE A POET

Fifty bucks to be a poet.
Fifty bucks to be a poet.
Hi, I'm Mrs. Sassy and
my brother is Mr. Bee.
So, how are you doing?
Come on, sit down.
Eat some cheese.
Drink something.

# BETWEEN FREE WILL
# AND DESTINY

We are God's
remote control dolls.
When we die,
He changes us
into new dolls.

But no matter what
happens to us,
God will love us
if we love
all His remote
control dolls.

# BLACK MOON

Papa is fishing
on black moon.
Black moon
is the moon
of fear and trouble,

But....

# WHITE MOON

is the moon of
peace.

White moon stops
all your troubles from
getting worse.

White moon
gives you the night
that warms your heart
with love.

# MOTHER EARTH

Grass  is Mother Earth's hair.
She is very hairy,
but on our lawn
she has some bald spots.
She has acorns for eyes
and sticks in her belly.
She looks funny,
but I still love her.

# BE A MAN

It took a long time
for him to turn
into a man,
time for him
to get a job...
and now
he sobs.

# PEPPERMINT TREE

Maybe I am.
Maybe Simon says
I'm not.

What is right.
What is wrong?
Do you think I'm cruel?

Or maybe not.
If Simon doesn't say I am,
I'm not.

I do not know because
Simon says nothing.

# SWITCH

Taking my head off
reversing it
with yours
to know
what you're thinking,
to know
what you know.

I like to reverse heads
with pigs!

# READY

I'm ready
to go
back
in my brain.
Good-bye.

OBSERVATIONS

# BAD BATTERIES

I have a stuffed unicorn
glowing in the dark,
glowing in daylight,
never stopping
from glowing.

It gives me headaches
until the batteries die.

# TORNADO WARNING

As I color,
crayons are walking
and there is a tornado
sucking all the crayons
into a colored
tornado

# THE BEACH IS NAKED TODAY

The beach
is naked today.
She forgot
to wear
her shell necklace
and she's swimming
with a crab.


# SOUNDS LIKE SPRING

Flowers are blooming.
Peppermint trees
are eating Altoids
and making funny faces.
It's all a masquerade song.

# RUNNING
## TO
### NOWHERE

Logan is running
to  nowhere.
Papa can't keep up.
Logan is running
too..ooo...ooo..ooo
FAST
so they fall
into nowhere.

# HEAD DOWN

1.

I tried to dance
but my flip-flops
were tired
of flip-flopping all day.
They made me trip
flip
and
flop.

2.

There's nothing
more boring
after soaring
than watching time
flip-flop
on a clock.

# RISING BACON

Pea pods,
a pinch of salt,
a pinch of bacon
and alt..
finishes the breakfast
for a big belly hawk.


# WAIT FOR ME

Designs on the wall
seem like magic
as I run down
with crayons running
with me
ending on
a picture..

# FUN

## AND

# LAUGHTER

# CHOCOLATE SCHOOL BUS

I was riding on
a chocolate school bus
taking me to Candy Lane School.

The candy-lane guards
stopped the bullies
from eating the bus.

They had to walk to school.
All the other children
had hot chocolate.

# STICKY CLEAN

Sticky, sticky hands,
sticky hands
all around
from the tree tops to the ground.


I washed my hands
inside my house

just to play with my
cat and mouse!

# ALL OF ME, HALF OF ME

An empty refrigerator
is a thermometer.

A picture frame without a picture
is just a file.

A pen without paper
is  only a pepper.

Why did the apple eat the seed?
Just to try for a new breed.

A lizard without colors
is a loser.

A mango with music
is a tango.

I'm a robot in the mood.
Don't you try to change my mood.

Why  have  a map
with no place to go?
          Answer the question!

# ZOO TRAIN

A zoo train
is a moo train.

Everyone will tell you
a Zoo Train
runs the moo line.

# GOOD NOTHING

The moon is mean
and green.
"Some children
love to scream,"
screamed Marlene...
What does that mean?
One time I lost my dream
because she was a witch.

# FROM FLORIDA WITH LOVE

I love to play
on the beach.
Everyone else
loves to screech.
Maybe because
they have no beach.

# THE SICK GHOST

Once I  was on the phone
with a ghost
when I heard him cough
and blow his nose.

He said he was sick.
He sneezed and he scoffed
and he fell down the stairs
and got tears in his ears.

"I'll go to a doctor,"
I heard  him say.
The doctor was mad
 and he blew him away.

# SAFE AND SOUND HORSE

My horse is my horse
and he's got three eyes.
He's made out of pillows
and feathers.

He has only two speeds.
He moves fast and slow.
It doesn't make sense,
I know, I know,
but I love my horse
with three eyes, just so.

# SQUASH

Rolie Polie guacamole
eating itself.
Rolie Polie guacamole
eating itself
because he's delicious
but doesn't want to die.

He wants to play squash
with his guacamole friends —
squishy squash
squishy squash.

# WHO NEEDS A QUEEN?

I'm  a bean
without a queen.

You can tease me.
You can scream.

I am strong and
you are wrong.

There's no need
for a queen bean.

# IN MY EYE

(A final thought)

You've got
your ear
in my eye.

and all that time
I was talking
to your mind

but so pleasant
is the sight of your
ear to my eye.

CPSIA information can be obtained
at www.ICGtesting.com
Printed in the USA
LVIC04n2345270315
432337LV00001B/1

9 781940 224725